# Vanished Away

## I Talk You Talk Press

Copyright © 2018 I Talk You Talk Press

ISBN: 978-4-907056-95-7

www.italkyoutalk.com

info@italkyoutalk.com

# CONTENTS

# 1. ON THE TRAIN

Satomi walked through the train. It was dark outside.

The front cars were full of passengers, but as she moved towards the back of the train there were fewer and fewer people.

*Where was Miki?* Her friend had picked up her purse and said she was going to the bathroom. That was an hour ago. She hadn't come back. Satomi tried calling her, but Miki's phone was turned off. *Was Miki sick? What had happened? Where was she?*

Satomi checked the bathrooms as she went. They were all empty.

Finally, she was in the last car. It was empty, and someone had turned off the lights. She saw a dim sign that said "bathrooms" at the far end. She felt her way towards it. Her leg touched something soft and silky. It was hair!

Shaking like a leaf, Satomi took out her mobile phone and turned on the light. A woman was lying across two seats, her head rolled back almost touching the floor. She let the light sweep over the young woman's face. It was not Miki. Satomi was sure this woman was dead. She turned and ran. She ran back towards the light and people.

In the third car back she found a conductor.

"Excuse me! Excuse me! There is a woman in the last car. I think she is dead!"

"Where?"

"I'll show you."

The conductor called his partner and they walked back. When they got to the door of the last car, Satomi couldn't go in. She

1

pointed. Her hand was shaking.

"In there."

One of the conductors turned on the lights. Satomi leant against the wall outside the car.

She could hear the men moving and talking quietly.

They came back. "I suppose you think it's a good joke. Telling us such lies," said one of the conductors. He was young, and looked annoyed.

Satomi stared. "What do you mean?"

"There's no one there. But of course you knew that, didn't you?"

"There was someone there. There was!"

The second conductor was older and kinder.

"Perhaps someone came back here to sleep. And now she's gone. You must have made a mistake. Perhaps she was sleeping and you woke her up. She left this scarf behind."

He pointed to the scarf in his colleague's hand.

Satomi raced to the door and looked in. There was no one there.

"Oh. I am so sorry. I was only looking for my friend. I don't know where she is. You must think I am crazy. Please forgive me."

"Go back to your seat. And don't go walking around the train again!" The first conductor looked angry.

"OK, I won't. I am so sorry."

The men started walking back and Satomi followed them. She was still shaking, and she was very, very worried.

*I won't go back to where we were sitting. I'll find another seat.* Satomi knew she must try to sort the puzzle out. The scarf the man had found belonged to Miki. The last time she had seen Miki, it had been around her neck.

*Miki must have been in the end carriage. She must have dropped it there. But that conductor is so angry with me, I can't say anything about the scarf to him. Anyway, he wouldn't believe me.*

## 2. WHO IS MIKI?

Satomi walked slowly, so that the men were well ahead of her. Then she looked around for an empty seat. There was an elderly woman sitting alone. Satomi sat down next to her. She pressed her hands to her face. Her head was aching. *What was happening?* Her head was full of questions.

She tried to think, but it was no good. She couldn't think of any answers, and she didn't know what to do. She leant her head back against the headrest and tried to relax. She thought about Miki. Miki had come to her school at the start of the year. They shared a dormitory room, and had become close friends. Miki was the best roommate Satomi had ever had, but were they really close? Miki was always happy, smiling and helpful. She was great at subjects like Japanese and history, but she was terrible at math. Since Satomi was good at math but hated writing essays, they helped each other a lot. But Satomi realized that she knew very little about her friend. She knew that she had come from Osaka, but Miki never spoke of her family or her past. Satomi didn't even know why she had changed schools. She had thought perhaps Miki had been bullied at her old school and that was why she never spoke of it. Miki had stayed at school during the summer vacation. She said that she had to study.

This trip was a first for Satomi. They were going to Okayama for the weekend. She had never been on vacation with a friend before. They had a hotel reservation and planned to go shopping and sightseeing. Miki had called it 'a post-exam present to ourselves'.

*But where was Miki?*

Satomi wondered whether she should find the conductors again and tell them Miki was missing.

Not a good idea. They had told her not to move around the train.

She could imagine their reaction if she went to them with another dramatic story. There was no chance they would believe her! Perhaps she could go to the police? Yes. She would go to the police in Okayama when the train arrived there. She was sure there would be some kind of police office near the railway station.

Making a decision made Satomi feel better. She closed her eyes and fell asleep.

Satomi woke up with a jump. She shook her head. As her eyes focused, she realised there was a cup of coffee in the cup holder in front of her seat.

"I'm pleased you woke up dear," said the woman next to her. "Your coffee must be almost cold."

"But where did it come from?" Satomi was puzzled.

"Oh, your boyfriend brought it for you about fifteen minutes ago. He said not to wake you up."

How could she have fallen asleep when Miki had disappeared and was maybe in trouble? Perhaps it was shock? She pulled out her phone and looked at it. She had only slept for about twenty minutes. Satomi picked up the plastic cup and took off the lid. There was something stuck to the underside of the lid. It was a small square of paper about the size of a postage stamp. She looked at it.

--- *Don't talk to anyone. Get off the train at Niimi* --- was written in tiny letters.

There was also a tiny heart and the letter "M". Satomi thought it looked like Miki's handwriting, but she couldn't be sure.

"Where is he now?" Satomi asked her neighbour.

"Oh, he came just before the train stopped at Nichinan. I think he got off there."

The train was slowing down. The woman next to Satomi wanted to get out of her seat. Satomi stood up to let her move.

"What station is this?" she asked the woman.

"Niimi".

Without stopping to think about it, Satomi picked up her purse and followed the women down the aisle. As she stood by the door, waiting to for the train to stop, she shivered. It was very cold.

# 3. INTO THE MOUNTAINS

The train stopped. Satomi got off the train, and stood on the platform, looking left and right. It was snowing. The train left. Satomi waited. Everyone else had moved away, and she was alone. She sighed and started walking towards the lights of the waiting room. Perhaps she could find the way to a police box from there.

A strong hand grabbed her arm and pulled her through a doorway, the other hand coming up to cover her mouth. She felt the man kick the door shut. Satomi tried to struggle, but the person was too strong.

"If you promise not to scream, I'll let you breathe."

She nodded.

"OK, then."

The man took his hand away from her mouth and grabbed her other arm. He stayed standing behind her. Satomi could feel his leather jacket. The voice sounded quite young.

"Miyu…, Miki, wants me to take you to her. I think it's a waste of time. We should have left you on the train. But I suppose after you talked to those conductors, we don't have a choice."

Satomi stopped feeling frightened and felt angry instead.

"What was I supposed to do? Anyway, there's no way I'm going with you anywhere! Let go of me!"

He released her arms. "OK, go! I'll tell Miki you wouldn't come."

Satomi turned around to face him. "Miki's my friend and I care about her!"

The room was lit by only one very dusty light. She couldn't see him well, but he was quite young. He wasn't much older than she was.

5

He was tall, with spiky hair and very bright eyes. He grinned at her.

"Seems Miki cares about you as well. I usually try to do what the lady wants. So, will you please come with me?"

Trying to think, Satomi looked away from him and around the room. It seemed to be some sort of storeroom.

"Uh… Yes I will. If you promise me you are really going to take me to Miki."

He laughed. "My promises aren't always worth much."

He grabbed her arm again.

"If you're coming, we've got to go. The longer we stay here the more danger you're in, and the more trouble I'm in."

Pulling her behind him, he opened the door quietly and edged along the wall of the station, keeping in the shadows. At the corner of the building he hissed in her ear, "See that tree over the far side of the car park? We have to run to there. When I say 'go', run!"

He looked around and seemed to be waiting for something. Satomi heard a train coming. As the train roared into the station, he pushed her. "Go!"

Satomi ran for the tree. He was close behind her. Behind the tree was a motorbike.

"Your transport, madam!"

He handed her a helmet. "I suppose you had better have this."

Satomi looked up at him. She sighed, but she put on the helmet. He took off his jacket.

"This too. If you get too cold you might fall off."

Wordlessly, Satomi put on the jacket and climbed onto the bike. The bike roared and they sped off into the snowy darkness.

The journey seemed to take forever. They soon left the town and took a wide road that went up into the hills. Then they rode along smaller roads that climbed on and on, up into the mountains. Finally the strange young man turned the bike onto a narrow gravel road that went down into a valley. Suddenly he turned the motorbike light and engine off. It was very dark, and Satomi didn't know how he could control the bike, or see where he was going.

After about three minutes, the bike slowly came to a stop. She climbed off the bike and staggered. She was cold and stiff.

"Wait here," he whispered in her ear.

He pushed the bike off the path and behind some bushes.

"This way. Don't make any noise!"

She followed him to some steps cut into the side of the hill. They climbed up and up. There were dead leaves all over the ground, and tall trees overhanging the steps. Finally, they came to a flat area. Satomi could just make out a shrine. It looked very old. He took her hand and led her over the rough ground to the back of the shrine. Almost hidden amongst the pine trees was an old house. The windows were all covered with heavy wooden shutters. They walked around the house. He stopped at a narrow door, pulled her close to him, and then very quickly, opened the door. Suddenly they were both inside. He closed the door behind them. The man took his boots off. Satomi kicked off her shoes. She took off the helmet and jacket and handed them to him. She followed him through an open door into a small room.

There was an old oil lamp hanging from the ceiling. Satomi looked around. It was a kitchen, and it looked like someone was still using it. There were some open packets of rice and tea and a kettle on an old oil stove.

"This way."

# 4. THE SWORD

They walked along a passageway in the dark towards a faint light shining through a crack between traditional sliding doors.

"In there."

He turned and walked back the way they had come. Satomi didn't want to slide the door open. Even though she had come all this way, she wasn't sure she really wanted to see Miki. She felt very angry. She put her face to the crack and looked in.

There was a futon in the middle of the room. Miki was kneeling next to it with her back to Satomi. Satomi knelt down and slid the door open. Miki turned round.

Her face was very pale, and she looked sad and exhausted. Satomi forgot her anger and threw herself at Miki. They hugged each other.

Miki was crying. "I'm so sorry! You have had a terrible time, and it's all my fault. But I couldn't tell you anything. I wanted to..."

Satomi hugged her harder. "It's all right. Don't worry."

She looked at the futon. There was a very tiny, very old man lying on it. He seemed to be asleep.

"This is my grandfather."

Miki knelt next to the futon again and stroked the old man's head.

"He can't hear us." She tucked the covers closely around him and motioned Satomi over to some cushions next to an oil heater that provided some heat.

"I'm going to explain and I hope you will forgive me."

Satomi was so puzzled, she couldn't stop the questions from coming out.

"Who was the boy with the motorbike? Who gave me the message on the train?"

"That was my brother, Tatsuya, and the biker was Yuta. I've known Yuta all my life. He's always got me into trouble, but this time he has got all of us in a terrible mess!"

"Hey, not so, Yuki! It wasn't all my fault this time! And anyway, aren't I getting you out of trouble?"

Yuta had entered the room silently, and was leaning against the wall with his arms folded. Miki pulled a face at him.

"I suppose he didn't introduce himself? Typical! Satomi, I'd like you to meet bad boy Yuta."

"How much are you going tell her?" asked Yuta.

"Everything!" said Miki firmly. "Tatsuya agrees."

He shrugged. "OK. Do it then. It makes a good story anyway." He slid down the wall and landed sitting cross-legged on the floor.

Miki looked down at her grandfather and stroked his face. She seemed to be gathering energy to speak.

"Miki. It's OK. You don't have to tell me anything."

She sighed. "I do. I owe it to you."

She sat back on her heels, and looked across at Satomi.

"Like Yuta says, it's a long story.

"There is a famous story, from the civil war in the fourteenth century. Masatsura was the son of a samurai, Masashige. When he was ten years old, he tried to kill himself with a sword that his father had given him. He was stopped, but his mother felt that the sword was evil and unlucky. She could not have it destroyed, because it was her husband's last gift to his son. So, she hid it. Later, she gave it to her eldest grandson when he became a warrior. It was never used, and over the years it passed from one generation to the other. A superstition grew that it must never be seen, so it was kept wrapped up and always hidden. It was a great heirloom. A great family treasure.

"Finally, it came into the possession of a priest, who was a direct descendant of Masatsura. He was the chief priest of a shrine in Kyushu, and so the sword was hidden there for a long time. When one chief priest died, the next one became the guardian, and so the knowledge was handed from one generation to the next, just like before.

"During the Second World War, the chief priest at the time became worried that Kyushu would be invaded. He thought that all the shrines would be destroyed, and the sword would be discovered. He had no close family to take over this responsibility, and he was getting old. So, he contacted an old school friend, who was also a distant relative, and told him the story. He asked him to help. The school friend was our mother's father, Tatsuya's and my grandfather. This is him." Miki turned to look at the old man, lying so still on the futon. She sighed, and continued.

"My grandfather knew that he would need help to take the sword and hide it. So, he asked if he could tell the secret to one more person, and the priest agreed. My grandfather told his greatest friend, Goemon Fujiwara. They went to Kyushu, took the sword and brought it here.

"This house, and the land around it, belongs to Fujiwara. They hid the sword very cleverly in the shrine in front of this house, so that no one would ever find it. After the war, my grandfather learnt that the priest had died. He felt that the responsibility was now his. Our family is also descended from Masatsura. When his son was old enough, our grandfather told him the secret, and life went on normally, until last year."

# 5. MIKI'S STORY

The old man moved slightly, and Miki leant back over him anxiously. The door opened, and a very handsome young man who looked a lot like Miki came in, carrying a tray.

"It must be hours since any of you ate. I've made some food and tea."

"Satomi, this is my big brother, Tatsuya."

Satomi smiled and said hello. He smiled back. He pulled a table away from the wall and put the tray on it. Yuta moved across the floor and joined them.

Yuta poured some tea into a cup and put some soup and rice into bowls. He took them across to Miki and knelt down next to her. While Tatsuya and Satomi ate and drank in silence, Yuta tried to get Miki to drink her tea and eat a little.

Then Miki continued. "So only three people knew about the sword. Our grandfather, Fujiwara, and our uncle. But then last year, our uncle died in an accident. Grandfather and Fujiwara were very old, and they worried about the future. So, Grandfather called a family conference. He had decided that we would all be told the secret, and that a younger person in the family would take responsibility for the sword. He thought it should go to a museum after his death. He had broken his promise to the priest in Kyushu, and it worried him. But he thought that life had changed, and this was the best thing he could do.

"We met in Osaka at New Year. Our grandfather, Fujiwara, Yuta, Tatsuya and I were there. Our parents died a long time ago. My grandfather had also asked his other granddaughter, Tomomi, to come. She was my uncle's only child.

"It was clear to me that my grandfather intended the sword to pass to Tatsuya, and that Tatsuya would present it to a museum as soon as my grandfather died. But Tomomi would not agree. She said she was the eldest, and the daughter of the only son. So, the sword was hers by right. Then her husband, Iwao arrived. Tomomi said it was her duty to tell him. Also, she said that since he had married into the family, and taken the family name, he must be given the sword."

There was a growling sound from Yuta, who was now lying on the floor beside the futon.

Miki looked tearful. She stopped talking. Tatsuya smiled. "Shall I explain some more?"

Miki nodded.

"Fujiwara was very angry. He tried to persuade our grandfather that Tomomi's husband could not be trusted. I don't think he knew anything then, but his instincts told him that Iwao was a bad man."

Yuta spoke from the floor. "Well, Granddad Fujiwara used to be a policeman. So he had seen plenty of criminals in his time. It turned out he was right."

Tatsuya went on. "Our grandfather is very traditional, and in some ways Tomomi was right, so he agreed. But he was very upset. He thought he had made a big mistake in telling us all about the sword. But he told Yuta and me to come here and take the sword from its hiding place in the shrine, and he gave it to Tomomi. Tomomi and Iwao went away. As soon as they had gone, our grandfather had a stroke. We got him to hospital and he stayed there until a few weeks ago.

"While our grandfather was ill in hospital, Fujiwara got Yuta to do some detective work. Yuta discovered that Iwao had married Tomomi and changed his name to try to get away from his debts. He's a gambler, and owes millions and millions of yen to a group of gangsters. The problem was that Tomomi really loved him. When Yuta went to see her, and told her about her husband's debts, she told Yuta she knew all about them. Worse. She had wanted the sword, so that Iwao could sell it to pay off his debts. She was really happy because Iwao had sent a message to the boss of the gangsters, and told them what he had. The boss had said he would accept the sword instead of money, so they didn't even have to sell it.

"Yuta gets angry very quickly. He argued with Tomomi, but she wouldn't listen. That night, Yuta waited until Iwao and Tomomi had gone out to celebrate. He got into their apartment, and stole the sword."

Miki started again. "Then we were all in trouble. Iwao and the gangsters were after Yuta. Tomomi isn't very clever, but she could guess who had stolen the sword. Worse, she told them all about us, so they were chasing Tatsuya, Fujiwara and me as well. I changed my name and moved schools. Tatsuya took Fujiwara to America. Yuta disappeared. He is the only one who knows where the sword is now, but the gangsters and Iwao don't know that."

Satomi shivered.

Tatsuya said, "I'll make more tea."

"Can you bring some cookies or something?" asked Yuta from the floor.

Tatsuya went out, and there was silence.

"Miki? Can I ask something?" Satomi's voice was small.

Miki turned to her friend.

"Is Yuta your cousin?"

"No, I'm not," Yuta answered for Miki.

"Then why did you go to the meeting? Why are you involved?"

"Oh," Miki managed a small laugh. "Sorry. Yuta is Fujiwara's grandson. So, he was told about the sword too. Grandfather raised Tatsuya and me, and poor Fujiwara had to bring up bad boy Yuta. We are all orphans. We grew up together. Even when we were older, we still spent summers together."

"Uh... and mm... what's your name? Yuta called you Yuki."

"He does sometimes. I'm Miyuki. That's why I chose Miki."

Satomi was very puzzled, but it did all make some strange kind of sense. It still didn't explain what had happened on the train, or why they were all in the closed-up house now. *I must remember to call Miki, Miyuki. That's her real name,* she thought.

Tatsuya came back with a new pot of tea. He tossed a bag of cookies to Yuta who reached out a hand and caught them. They waited while Yuta ate a couple of cookies, and then he told Satomi more of the story.

"Tatsuya got my granddad, that's Fujiwara, to San Francisco safely. Then they tried to make a plan to solve the problem. Granddad was quite famous when he was younger. He was head of the police in

13

Okayama. And he still has a lot of connections with the police and other people. They worked out a deal with a museum here in Japan, but it took months. They wanted a lot of information to prove that the sword was really the sword of Masashige. It was more difficult because they were in America. Also, they had to hide the fact that I had stolen the sword, and that they didn't know where I was, or even where the sword was. Granddad found out from his old friends in the police that Tomomi never reported the theft of the sword. Probably she was worried they'd take too much notice of Iwao. Still, there was a chance that if we told everyone, Tomomi would say something.

"Meanwhile, I was moving from place to place and Miyuki was the go-between. We decided to talk to Tomomi, so Miyuki contacted her. Tomomi was very frightened. I don't think she had ever realized how dangerous the gangsters were. They had threatened her, and she thought they might kill her. Also, she discovered that Iwao was having an affair with another woman. He had hit her and threatened to kill her if she didn't get the sword back. She wanted to get away from the gangsters and she wanted to get away from her husband."

He laughed. "Tomomi didn't change completely though. She wasn't worried about them killing me. And believe me, if they had found me, they would have. If Iwao didn't kill me first!"

Miyuki looked tearful again, and put her hand on Yuta's shoulder. "I'll explain what happened next."

"Tomomi said she would go along with the plan, if we would help her to hide. She wanted to go to America. Of course, she didn't know that Tatsuya and Fujiwara were already there. Fujiwara asked some old friends to help."

"They were probably criminals from the old days," said Yuta cheerfully.

"Anyway," Miyuki continued. "Somehow Fujiwara got her a false passport and a visa. Then we had to find a way of getting them to her. She said she would only meet with me. She didn't like Yuta for some reason!"

Yuta smiled. "I didn't like her either!"

"So, we made a plan. Tomomi would tell Iwao that she planned to visit an old family friend in Okayama, who might know where Yuta was. She would tell him the friend would only talk to her. Then I would meet her on the train. I would give her the passport, and she would disappear by flying from Okayama to China, and then on to America. Tatsuya got air tickets for her, and everything seemed fine."

Miyuki looked at Satomi. "I know it seems like I was using you. And I guess I was. But I needed some normal reason to be on the train. I thought it would be safe and easy. And then I could relax with you in Okayama. We would have a great weekend, and I could think about getting my life back."

"It's OK," said Satomi slowly. Her head was buzzing as she thought about the strange story. "You have been in danger since January. You have been hiding. I think I understand. But was it Tomomi on the train? What happened to her? And why are we in this house?"

# 6. DANGER EVERYWHERE

Yuta suddenly rose to his feet in a single movement. He put his fingers to his mouth to signal that everyone must be quiet. Then he slipped out of the room. Tatsuya followed, leaving Miyuki and Satomi alone with the sick, old man.

Miyuki leaned over him as though she could protect him with her body. Satomi stayed perfectly still and quiet. She was very frightened.

Miyuki and Satomi stared at each other. They seemed to wait for a long time.

There was a sound outside the room and both of them jumped. Tatsuya appeared at the door.

"It's OK. Yuta heard something outside, and we went to look. We are all worried that Tomomi knew about this place. She might have told Iwao and the gangsters. Yuta thinks it is only a matter of time before they turn up here. He thinks they might be watching it and waiting."

"He might be right, but this time it was only a tanuki. We usually don't see them in winter, but maybe this one got disturbed."

"So there could be someone out there?" Satomi was unhappy.

Tatsuya shrugged. "Maybe. But Yuta and I couldn't see anything."

"Why did you come here? Why didn't you go somewhere safer? Somewhere near a police station?" Satomi was confused.

"We all know this house well. When we were children, we spent every summer here," explained Miyuki. "Fujiwara told us not to trust the police. We couldn't tell them the whole story. And, anyway, some of them are gamblers too. The gangsters can get information from

16

the police very easily. But we only came here because of our grandfather.

"At the same time as we were making plans with Tomomi, Grandfather seemed to be getting a little better. The gangsters had been watching the hospital, so they knew as well. There was a chance they might find out that he could talk sometimes. That meant they might try to attack him in the hospital. Tatsuya came back from America. He and Yuta got grandfather out of the hospital and brought him here. We thought it was safer, and also it is very familiar to him. He was a lot better and happier for a few days. But we were too optimistic. He had another stroke, and now he is sicker than before. A neighbour who lives down in the valley moved in to help care for him. She is a nurse. We have known her for years and we call her Aunty. We asked her to go home, just before Yuta brought you here. We were worried she might be in danger too."

"Okay," said Satomi. "But I'm sorry. I am so confused. What happened? Where did the plan go wrong?"

"Tatsuya sent the passport and tickets to me at school. He and Yuta weren't happy because I was going to meet Tomomi alone. So they caught the train as well. I went to meet Tomomi in the back carriage, but when I got there, she was dead. Tatsuya and Yuta were waiting in the next carriage. We decided I had to get off the train. Tatsuya called our neighbour's husband from the train and asked him to drive down and get us. Then Tatsuya and I got off at the next stop. But I was thinking of you too. If Iwao had seen you with me, you might be in danger too. So Tatsuya found you and left you my message."

"But if that was Tomomi, what happened to her?"

"We think Iwao followed her, and saw Miyuki on the train," said Tatsuya. "He guessed what she was going to do and killed her."

"Okay," said Satomi slowly. "But where did her body go?"

"Oh, that was me!" Yuta stood up and strolled over to the door. "I was standing behind the door of the carriage when you came in. I had just enough time to move her, before you came back with the conductors."

"Where....?"

"In the bathroom of course. Couldn't have them finding her. No one would have been allowed off the train. Of course they'll find her when they clean the train in Okayama."

Satomi thought she had never met anyone like Yuta before, but she thought she liked Tatsuya more. He was much kinder.

"I'm going to bed," said Yuta. "See you in the morning." He disappeared out the door.

Tatsuya stood up too. "Is Satomi going to sleep in your room?"

"I hope so," replied Miyuki. Just then an elderly woman came into the room. Miyuki stood up, and for the first time that night, Satomi saw Miyuki smile.

"Oh, Aunty. Thank you for coming back. He is about the same I think."

"Of course he is, dear!" said the woman hugging Miyuki. "I'll watch him tonight. You and your friend should get some sleep. You both look exhausted."

Miyuki kissed her grandfather and then motioned to Satomi. They left the room.

"My old bedroom here is freezing cold. But at least we can have a good bath. There's lots of hot water. Aunty's husband keeps the wood burner going."

She opened another sliding door. There was an oil lamp and another heater, but it was still dark and cold. Satomi and Miyuki's bags were by the door.

Miyuki saw that Satomi was surprised. "Tatsuya knew where we were sitting. He rescued our bags when he delivered the message to you, before he and I got off the train."

The bathroom was very old, but as Miyuki had promised the water was hot. After a bath, they put out futons and lay down.

Miyuki giggled, "It's a bit different from the hotel we were planning in Okayama, isn't it?"

Satomi did not answer. She was already asleep.

# 7. THE NEXT DAY

Satomi woke up. She had no idea what time it was, because the wooden shutters blocked out the light. She looked at her phone. It was 11:00am! Miyuki was not there. She dressed and went to the kitchen.

The others were sitting at the table. They had eaten, and it seemed they had been up for hours.

"Good morning! There's tea and you can make toast if you want it." Miyuki seemed cheerful.

Satomi got herself some breakfast and joined them at the table.

Yuta reached out and stole a piece of Satomi's toast.

He spoke with his mouth full. "Everything is organized. If we're lucky, I'll be able to lead a normal life again after tonight!"

"Your life's never normal!" laughed Miyuki.

Tatsuya leaned back in his chair and explained.

"Now that Tomomi's dead, we can go ahead with grandfather's original plan. Of course, he wanted us to wait until after he died, but we don't see any reason to do that now. Yuta's grandfather agrees. We talked with him in San Francisco. Only the gangsters and Iwao know that Tomomi ever had the sword, or that Yuta stole it. We need to persuade the gangsters that there is no reason to chase us anymore. If we don't have the sword – why would they chase us?"

"So Yuta and I will take the sword to the museum. Then we will tell the gangsters what we have done."

"Won't that be dangerous?" asked Satomi. "If they are very angry, they might still attack you for revenge."

Yuta shrugged. "They will go after Iwao, not us. They are businessmen. And we have some insurance."

"Insurance?" asked Satomi.

Tatsuya explained. "We have been talking to Fujiwara's old friend, Mr Takada, this morning. He was Chief of Police for Southwest Japan, when Fujiwara was working in Okayama. He is going to help. He will come with us to the museum, and then when we go to see the gangsters. The gangsters know him. They don't like him, but they trust him. He has arranged for the police to send a car for us. We will be well protected."

"What about Iwao?" Satomi thought they were all too cheerful and calm. "Didn't he murder Tomomi?"

"We think so," said Miyuki. "The railway cleaners found her body last night. The police identified her. We think Iwao killed her, but none of us saw him on the train. We have no proof. We talked to the police, and they say they can question Iwao, but they don't think they can do anything. Mr Takada says it's better to leave it to his enemies. Either they will find him and kill him, or he will be so busy running and hiding from them, he will have no time to think about any of us."

She looked at the clock. "The car will be here in ten minutes. You had better hurry."

"Yuta. Where is the sword?"

"We'll pick it up at the bottom of the steps. No worries!"

The men picked up their jackets and went outside. Satomi and Miyuki followed them. They walked down the steps, back to the narrow road. Yuta went behind the bushes and got his motor bike. Satomi noticed that the front forks were very long. The front wheel was a long way in front of the handlebars. "I had my bike altered specially," grinned Yuta. "It's clever isn't it?"

He pulled at the front fork. There was a stainless steel covering that came away. The fork was hollowed out. Inside was a long steel tube. He pulled it out and handed it to Tatsuya, just as a big black shiny car arrived. A very distinguished old man got out. He hugged Miyuki and shook hands with the two young men. No one said anything. The three men got into the car and it drove away.

Miyuki and Satomi waved. Then in silence they climbed up the steps back to the house.

It was a long strange and lonely day. Miyuki spent her time

helping their neighbour to care for her grandfather. Miyuki was quiet and pale. Although she had been cheerful earlier, it was obvious that she was very worried. Satomi found some books to read, but couldn't concentrate.

Finally, at about 5:30pm, she heard voices. Satomi rushed outside with Miyuki. Tatsuya and Yuta were outside. They were both smiling.

"Everything went well!" shouted Yuta.

"Was it OK with the gangsters?" asked Miyuki.

"No problem. The boss was a very nice guy. He thought I had talent and offered me a job!"

Tatsuya looked across at Satomi and smiled.

"It really was OK. Mostly due to Mr Takada."

They walked into the house and went to the grandfather's room Miyuki knelt down and whispered for a long time to the old man. It was impossible to know if he could hear her or not, but Satomi thought perhaps a very faint smile crossed his face.

# 8. BACK TO SCHOOL

Miyuki had cooked curry and rice for them all. Everyone was relaxing when Satomi suddenly shouted.

"School! The train!"

Miyuki laughed. "I wondered when you would remember that! We've got plenty of time. You can catch it at Niimi at eight. Tatsuya can borrow Aunty's husband's car and take you there. We're all coming to see you off."

"How about you? Aren't you coming too?"

Miyuki shrugged. "I'm not going back. I'll stay here with Tatsuya, until Grandfather dies. I don't think he will live much longer, and we don't want to move him again."

So Satomi found herself back on the platform of Niimi Station. Miyuki hugged her and promised to text every day. "And I will come to see you very soon."

As Satomi went to get on the train, she suddenly felt very lonely. She would miss Miyuki's company at school. She looked across at Miyuki. She and Yuta were standing together. It was obvious, however much they argued, that they loved each other very much. Tatsuya saw her looking at them.

"The grandfathers have always hoped that they will marry. Yuta is improving a lot. He is not as crazy as he was. So maybe."

Satomi smiled at Tatsuya. He was holding something behind his back. He handed it to her with a smile.

"A drink for the train." It was a container of coffee.

She took her seat, the train left and she waved until the three of them could no longer be seen.

She was still holding the cup of coffee. There was a piece of paper stuck to the bottom of the cup. She put the cup in the holder and unfolded the note.

--- *See you, Tatsuya* ---

Satomi smiled, held the note in her hand and fell asleep.

# THANK YOU

Thank you for reading Vanished Away! We hope you enjoyed the story. (Word count: 6,700)

If you would like to read more graded readers, please visit our website
http://www.italkyoutalk.com

Other Level 4 graded readers include
Chi-obaa and Friends
Chi-obaa and Her Town
End House (Old Secrets – Modern Mysteries Book 2)
On the Run (Old Secrets – Modern Mysteries Book 3)
The Blue Lace Curtain (Old Secrets – Modern Mysteries Book 1)
The Legacy
The Witches of Nakashige

# ABOUT THE AUTHOR

I Talk You Talk Press is a Japan-based publisher of language textbooks, graded readers and language learning/teaching resources.

Our team is made up of highly experienced language teachers and translators, who have all studied at least one additional language to an advanced level.

This experience enables us to design our materials from the perspective of both the teacher and the learner. We consult with both teachers and language learners when designing our textbooks and graded readers, and test our materials extensively in the classroom before publication.

We are a fast-growing press, and currently publish graded readers for learners of English. We publish new graded readers monthly.

www.ingramcontent.com/pod-product-compliance
Lightning Source LLC
Chambersburg PA
CBHW022352040426
42449CB00006B/842